The Almost Chosen People

Books By William J. Wolf

MAN'S KNOWLEDGE OF GOD

NO CROSS, NO CROWN:
A Study of the Atonement

THE ALMOST CHOSEN PEOPLE:
A Study of the Religion of Abraham Lincoln

THE ALMOST CHOSEN PEOPLE

A Study of the Religion of Abraham Lincoln

By William J. Wolf

Howard Chandler Robbins Professor
Episcopal Theological School

DOUBLEDAY & COMPANY, INC.

Garden City, New York

1959

Library of Congress Catalog Card Number 59-12662

Printed in the United States of America
First Edition

To my wife ELEANOR
and to our boys
EDWIN, JOHN, and STEPHEN

CONTENTS

Chapter 1

"I Made a Solemn Vow before God" *17*

Chapter 2

"In a Twilight, Feeling and Reasoning My Way" *33*

Chapter 3

"Stand Still, *and See the Salvation of the Lord"* *55*

Chapter 4

"Now Convinced of the Truth of the Christian Religion" *69*

Chapter 5

"Stamped with the Divine Image and Likeness" 89

Chapter 6

"An Humble Instrument in the Hands of the Almighty" 115

Chapter 7

"The Best Gift God Has Given to Man" 131

Chapter 8

1862—"The Will of God Prevails" 143

Chapter 9

1863—"This Nation, under God" 161

Chapter 10

1864–65—"With Malice toward None,
With Charity for All,
With Firmness in the Right" 173

Appendix I Creed of Abraham Lincoln *195*

Appendix II Bibliography *197*

Footnotes and References *201*

Index

The title of this book has been adapted from Lincoln's address to the New Jersey Senate at Trenton on February 21, 1861. After describing the impression made upon him as a boy by the accounts of the Revolutionary Battles in New Jersey from Weem's *Life of Washington,* Lincoln continued:

"I recollect thinking then, boy even though I was, that there must have been something more than common that those men struggled for. I am exceedingly anxious that that thing which they struggled for; that something even more than National Independence; that something that held out a great promise to all the people of the world to all time to come; I am exceedingly anxious that this Union, the Constitution, and the liberties of the people shall be perpetuated in accordance with the original idea for which that struggle was made, and I shall be most happy indeed if I shall be an humble instrument in the hands of the Almighty, and of this, his almost chosen people, for perpetuating the object of that great struggle." (*Collected Works of Abraham Lincoln, IV, p. 236*)

The Almost Chosen People

"I Made a Solemn Vow before God"

Chapter 1

It was September 22, 1862. The President's Cabinet was in session to consider an urgent problem on which Lincoln wanted advice. Secretary of the Treasury Salmon Chase had just asked the President to repeat what he had been saying. Lincoln had described his decision to emancipate the slaves in territories then in rebellion against the federal government. Toward the end the President's voice had become lower and more solemn. Secretary Chase wanted to be certain he had understood Lincoln's words. The President repeated:

"I made a solemn vow before God, that if General Lee was driven back from Pennsylvania, I would crown the result by the declaration of freedom to the slaves."[1]

At times writers have not reported this incident in their accounts of the cabinet session. Many omit the specific statement of Lincoln about a "solemn vow before God" and describe instead "a solemn resolution." This, however, is to substitute a black and white photograph with blurred focus for the rich colors of a masterpiece. The problem is not one of historical evidence. Few incidents in Lincoln's life are so well documented as this one. The quotation used is from the artist Francis Carpenter, who lived in the White House at the President's invitation as he worked on his painting of the reading of the Proclamation. Carpenter interviewed all who were present at the event and has recorded the most minute particulars in his famous book published in 1866. Had they found any inaccuracy the members of the Cabinet might have challenged him at this early date.

In addition to Carpenter's careful records there are at least two accounts from the diaries of cabinet members. The first is the statement of Secretary Chase:

"The President then took a graver tone, and said, Gentlemen: I have, as you are aware, thought a great deal about the relation of this war to slavery; and you all remember that, several weeks ago, I read to you an order I had prepared on this subject, which, on account of objections made by some of you, was not issued. Ever since then my mind has been much occupied with this subject, and I have thought, all along, that the time for acting on it might probably come. I think the time has come now. I wish it were a better time. I wish that we were in a better condition. The action of the army against the rebels has not been quite what I should best like. But they have been driven out of Maryland, and Pennsylvania is no longer in danger of invasion. When the Rebel Army was at Frederick, I determined, as soon as it should be driven out of Maryland, to issue a Proclamation of Emancipation, such as I thought most likely to be useful. I said nothing to anyone, but I made a promise to myself, and (hesitating a little) to my Maker. The Rebel Army is now driven out, and I am going to fulfill that promise."[2]

The second confirmation comes from the diary of Gideon Welles, the Secretary of the Navy:

"We have a special Cabinet meeting. The subject was the Proclamation concerning emancipating slaves. . . . There were some differences in the Cabinet, but he had formed his own conclusions, and made his own decisions. He had, he said, made a vow, a covenant, that if God gave us the victory in the approaching battle (which had just been fought) he would consider it his duty to move forward in the cause of emancipation. We might think it strange, he said, but there were times when he felt uncertain how to act; that he had in this way submitted the disposal of matters when the way was not clear to his mind what he should do. God had decided this question in favor of the slave. He was satisfied it was right—was confirmed and strengthened by the vow and its results; his mind was fixed, his decision made; but he wished his paper announcing his course to be as correct in terms as it could be made without any attempt to change his determination. For that was fixed."[3]

The testimony is incontrovertible. Lincoln reached his decision about the timing of the Proclamation in an immediate awareness of the presence of God. For Lincoln, God was not a "cosmic blur," nor the parsons' "stock in trade," nor the politicians' benediction over spread-eagle oratory. God was ultimate yet personal reality, and He made Himself accessible to one who sought Him out. For Lincoln, God was the final court of appeal when he was uncertain about the moral aspects of a question. God's guidance was sought when Lincoln wanted to pass through the tides of political expediency to stand on bedrock.

One is prompted to ask why in traditional accounts of this cabinet session many historians have omitted the very key to understanding it. They would probably reply that their task is to show the sociological, political, and economic factors in the evolution of Lincoln's attitude toward emancipation. Their studies are of course tremendously valuable in just this area. They bring a needed corrective to the mythological picture of the young flatboater in New Orleans vowing to crush "that thing" and there and then charting a course toward the White House with abolitionist banner flying.

We can better understand Lincoln's final act of emancipation when we realize that for long he was balked by a dilemma. He believed that despite the moral wrong of slavery the federal government was prevented by the Constitution from disturbing it in the original states. He had early accepted the Missouri Compromise as a practical way of getting along between North and South. It was the upsetting of this balance by the passage of the Kansas-Nebraska Act that drew Lincoln again into the political arena. He felt called to oppose Douglas's doctrine of "popular sovereignty" by which territories would themselves determine whether to enter the federal Union as slave or as free states. In his early years as President, Lincoln held off the abolitionists with his argument that he was sworn to defend the Union. Only, it seemed, as an act of military necessity could he free the slaves in the conviction that a technically unconstitutional step might be needed to preserve the Union itself.

The sequence of events just before Lincoln's decision is interesting. Horace Greeley attempted to dictate to Lincoln in an open letter in the *Tribune* entitled "The Prayer of Twenty Millions" and demanded immediate emancipation. Lincoln stated his position with forceful clarity in a letter to the editor on August 22, 1862.

"My paramount object in this struggle *is* to save the Union, and is *not* either to save or to destroy slavery. If I could save the Union without freeing *any* slave I would do it, and if I could save it by freeing *all* the slaves I would do it; and if I could save it by freeing some and leaving others alone, I would also do that. What I do about slavery, and the colored race, I do because I believe it helps to save the Union; and what I forbear, I forbear because I do *not* believe it would help to save the Union. I shall do *less* whenever I shall believe what I am doing hurts the cause, and I shall do *more* whenever I shall believe doing more will help the cause. I shall try to correct errors when shown to be errors; and I shall adopt new views so fast as they shall appear to be true views.

"I have here stated my purpose according to my view of *official* duty; and I intend no modification of my oft-expressed *personal* wish that all men everywhere could be free."[4]

Three weeks later he was waited upon by two clergymen who presented a memorial from a mass meeting of Chicago Christians of all denominations. He listened to the document, which demanded immediate emancipation, and then replied with a firmness probably stiffened by his distaste for the oversimplification of a very complex issue:

"I am approached with the most opposite opinions and advice, and that by religious men, who are equally certain that they represent the divine will. I am sure that either the one or the other class is mistaken in that belief, and perhaps in some respects both. I hope it will not be irreverent for me to say that if it is probable that God would reveal his will to others, on a point so connected with my duty, it might be supposed he would reveal it directly to me; for, unless I am more deceived in myself than I often am, it is my earnest desire to know the will of Providence in this matter. *And if I can learn what it is, I will do it!* These are not, however, the days of miracles, and I suppose it will be granted that I am not to expect a direct revelation. I must study the plain, physical facts of the case, ascertain what is possible and learn what appears to be wise and right. The subject is difficult, and good men do not agree."

He then spoke of division in a New York delegation that had been to see him and of perplexity in the last Congress, even though the majority were anti-slavery. He pointedly went on:

"Why, the rebel soldiers are praying with a great deal more earnestness, I fear, than our own troops, and expecting God to favor their side; for one of our soldiers, who had been taken prisoner, told Senator Wilson, a few days since, that he met with nothing so discouraging as the evident sincerity of those he was among in their prayers."

Lincoln then analyzed the pros and cons of the proposal and invited a reply. The two clergymen replied point by point in an hour of earnest discussion. The interview ended with the President saying:

"Do not misunderstand me, because I have mentioned these objections. They indicate the difficulties that have thus far prevented my action in some such way as you desire. I have not decided against a proclamation of liberty to the slaves, but hold the matter under advisement. And I can assure you that the subject is on my mind, by day and night, more than any other. Whatever shall appear to be God's will I will do. I trust that, in the freedom with which I have canvassed your views, I have not in any respect injured your feelings."[5]

At the end of the week following the visit of the Chicago delegation Lincoln summoned his Cabinet. He was ready to issue a proclamation freeing most of the slaves, but first, heeding Seward's earlier advice, he had wanted a victory such as Antietam. He did not want the act to be interpreted as the despairing gesture of a sorely pressed government. Also he had been seeking to submit this question to higher authority, to the God Who, he firmly believed, presided over man's history and Who acted within that history, even if His will might be difficult for man to understand. By the date of the cabinet session Lincoln was convinced that "God had decided this question in favor of the slave. He was satisfied it was right—was confirmed and strengthened by the vow and its results."

Clearly Lincoln's motivation in this historic act had much more to it than politics or military necessity. His decision was not made "apart" from these factors, in a vacuum of the soul, but "beyond" them. This "transhistorical" dimension in Lincoln illuminates the course of history itself. Historians by their conventional methods describe events as a chemist might analyze the pigmentation on a masterpiece. It was given to Lincoln, however, in a uniquely imaginative way to stand at the perspective from which the divine artist paints his canvas and to help others to appreciate that masterpiece.

In this sense Lincoln is one of the greatest theologians of America—not in the technical meaning of producing a system of doctrine, certainly not as the defender of some one denomination, but in the sense of seeing the hand of God intimately in the affairs of nations. Just so the prophets of Israel criticized the events of their day from the perspective of the God Who is concerned for history and Who reveals His will within it. Lincoln stands among God's latter-day prophets.

Although many Christians in his time tried to describe God's judgments in history they usually produced a wooden and unconvincing oversimplification. It ministered to the self-righteousness of the one making the judgment. An obvious case in point was the doctrinaire theory of the abolitionists that every evil in America stemmed from Southern slaveholders. Lincoln saw the complexity of historical processes, the mixture of human motivations, and man's incurable self-righteousness. All three bedevil human history. For Lincoln, God's judgments were enacted organically within history rather than forced upon it mechanically from without.

This can best be illustrated by his view of the moral question in slavery, which became ever clearer to him after his debates with Douglas. The country was founded upon the belief expressed in the Declaration of Independence that all men were created equal. Slavery was a living lie in contradicting that fundamental principle which for Lincoln had the force of divine revelation. The Civil War he came to understand as the punishment visited by God upon a nation denying its true destiny by its refusal to put slavery "in process of ultimate extinction." The war came as the final organic breakdown within the nation of this built-in contradiction to the law of its life. Lincoln would never have denied the political, psychological, and economic causes of the Civil War. Indeed, he could articulate them sharply, but he pressed beyond them to see the whole sweep of the nation's history in terms of God's judgments and mercies. Lincoln saw American history in the freshness of prophetic insight. He is the American Isaiah, or Jeremiah, or St. Paul.

This book will attempt to explore this "transhistorical" dimension in Lincoln and to show how it complements rather than negates the important historical studies of recent years. It will try to show how Lincoln's living awareness of God helped him resolve his ethical dilemmas ("there were times when he felt uncertain how to act") and take responsible action "with firmness in the right, as God gives us to see the right" and yet "with charity for all."

It would be unfair, however, to reproach careful historians for not giving us all the story behind the Proclamation of Emancipation, if one did not offer some justification for their shying away from the religious dimension in Lincoln. There developed immediately after his death a religion about Lincoln as "the dying God." This cult has been scrutinized provocatively by Lloyd Lewis in *Myths after Lincoln.* The mythologized picture was soon read back into the day-to-day events of his life to the utter confusion of the historical record. Against this tissue of legend the critical historians of Lincoln have rightly protested.

Many members of the Christian community, moreover, have added to the confusion. They have been shameless in claiming Lincoln as a secret member of their denomination or about to become such. Many parsons sought publicity and self-glorification in their accounts of supposed conversations with Lincoln. Others, like Father Chiniquy, who did have interviews put the most improbable speeches into Lincoln's mouth. The conflicting evidence on Lincoln's religion is incredibly complex. One could "prove" about anything by selecting what he wanted from the sources. The fair-minded investigator must finally admit that the only really reliable testimony, with a few exceptions, must be gleaned from Lincoln's own speeches and letters. This central core of authentic Lincoln utterance in the Rutgers edition of his works must be the acid test for other supplementary evidence critically evaluated.

An example of the caution that must be exercised is provided by the famous "Beecher incident," which snowballed from nothing into a pious tale widely circulated by uncritical writers. Dr. Chapman accepted its authenticity in his *Latest Light on Lincoln,* claiming that "upon the scene of this unique event there rests a halo of celestial beauty too sacred to be regarded with indifference or doubt."

According to a grandson of Henry Ward Beecher who claimed to have heard it from Mrs. Beecher "in her old age," Lincoln after the disaster of Bull Run appeared at their Brooklyn door with his face hidden in a military cloak. Without giving his name he asked to see the famous preacher. The anxious Mrs. Beecher at her husband's bidding admitted the suspicious character. Behind closed doors she heard their voices and the pacing of their feet until the mysterious visitor left about midnight. Shortly before Beecher's death he is supposed to have revealed that his caller was Lincoln in disguise.

"Alone for hours that night, like Jacob of old, the two had wrestled together in prayer with the God of battles and the Watcher over the right until they had received the help which He had promised to those that seek His aid."[6]

While it is unthinkable that the President would have stolen away secretly from Washington at a time of national crisis when he might just as well have summoned Beecher to Washington if he wanted to see him, the story still has its defenders. The really decisive evidence against it was provided by Beecher himself. Along with others, he was asked to contribute reminiscences of Lincoln to the *North American Review*. He never described anything remotely resembling this Nicodemus visit and said he really did not know Lincoln very well personally!

Even highly respected members of the Christian community have fallen into serious error by accepting the accounts of others in good faith but with historical naïveté. There is a famous example of this with respect to the cabinet meeting under discussion. Bishop Charles Henry Fowler devoted some one hundred pages to Lincoln in his *Patriotic Orations*, published in 1910. The speech had its origin in a funeral eulogy delivered in Chicago on May 4, 1865, and was repeated by popular request hundreds of times over more than thirty years.

Bishop Fowler had heard that at the beginning of the cabinet meeting Lincoln read from a book. What book could it be? Either Bishop Fowler caught the suggestion from another pious source or he supplied what he thought was the appropriate book for such a momentous occasion. Bishop Fowler said he read a chapter from the Bible. Secretary Chase wrote that he read a chapter from the humorist Artemus Ward on "A High-Handed Outrage at Utica."

What is plainly needed in the exploration of Lincoln's religion is the historian's rigorous rejection of the mythologized picture and yet an honest wrestling with the irreducible religious core that illuminates his acts. It may even be that Lincoln's humor throws some light upon his religious faith. This would not have been understood by the humorless and pompous Chase, who reported of the cabinet session: ". . . [Lincoln] proposed to read a chapter which he thought very funny. Read it, and seemed to enjoy it very much."

There is still another problem about Lincoln's religion that has been a source of embarrassment to many people. They are worried about anyone taking such a vow as Lincoln made. They object that this reduces man's relationship to God to a transactional level. ("I'll free the slaves if You, God, will give us victory.") They argue that it savors of primitive superstition and has no place in a reasoned faith. Both dangers are obviously serious ones and could prove fatal in the hands of a fanatic or even of a lesser man. The element that rescues Lincoln is the integrity of his vision of God's will and his unself-righteous perspective on himself. Lincoln's view of reality had, however, an element of the primitive in it represented by the vow and also by his interest in dreams as foretelling the future.

Lamon has recorded the dream that came to Lincoln shortly before his death and claims that his recollection of Lincoln's words was based on notes taken just after the event. Lincoln dreamed that he heard invisible mourners in the White House. He explored until in the East Room he saw a catafalque with a corpse guarded by soldiers. "Who is dead in the White House?" he demanded of one. "The President," came the reply; "he was killed by an assassin!" Turning to Mrs. Lincoln, Lamon, and the others present, Lincoln added:

"It seems strange how much there is in the Bible about dreams. There are, I think, some sixteen chapters in the Old Testament and four or five in the New in which dreams are mentioned . . . If we believe the Bible, we must accept the fact that in the old days God and His angels came to men in their sleep and made themselves known in dreams. Nowadays dreams are regarded as very foolish, and are seldom told, except by old women and by young men and maidens in love. . . . After it occurred, the first time I opened the Bible, strange as it may appear, it was at the twenty-eighth chapter of Genesis, which related the wonderful dream Jacob had. I turned to other passages, and seemed to encounter a dream or a vision wherever I looked. I kept on turning the leaves of the old book, and everywhere my eye fell upon passages recording matters strangely in keeping with my own thoughts,—supernatural visitations, dreams, visions, etc."[7]

This resort to a vow, the concern about dreams, and some inquiries into spiritualism were survivals of the primitive biblicism and backwoods superstition that characterized frontier religion. While this influence was undoubtedly strong on Lincoln, there is the opposite side of him with its highly rational criticism of popular religion. In the incident with which we began this chapter it is important to note Lincoln's words that the vow "confirmed and strengthened" *his own decision*. It did not magically replace that careful weighing of evidence and logical analysis which is so characteristically a part of his perennial appeal. This side of his nature he expressed to the Chicago clergymen: "I suppose . . . I am not to expect a direct revelation. I must study the plain, physical facts of the case, ascertain what is possible and learn what appears to be wise and right."

It is clear that Lincoln's religion had many facets. Only caricature can result from seizing upon one element within the complex and neglecting to evaluate other significant and modifying factors. The simplest description of his religion would be "singlehearted integrity in humbly seeking to understand God's will in the affairs of men and his own responsibility therein." The development of that religion and its expression in his life will be the subject of this study. Lincoln's simplicity of purpose and his religious awareness have been movingly expressed by Stephen Vincent Benét in a poetic paraphrase of Lincoln's own words.

What is God's will?

They come to me and talk about God's will
In righteous deputations and platoons,
Day after day, laymen and ministers.
They write me Prayers From Twenty Million Souls
Defining me God's will and Horace Greeley's.
God's will is General This and Senator That,
God's will is those poor colored fellows' will,

It is the will of the Chicago churches,
It is this man's and his worst enemy's.
But all of them are sure they know God's will.
I am the only man who does not know it.

And, yet, if it is probable that God
Should, and so very clearly, state His will
To others on a point of my own duty,
It might be thought He would reveal it me
Directly, more especially as I
So earnestly desire to know His will.[8]